America's Story:

The History
of the

Pledge of Allegiance

Tricia Raymond

AMERICA'S STORY:
THE HISTORY OF THE
PLEDGE OF ALLEGIANCE

BY

TRICIA RAYMOND

www.libertyaloud.com

ISBN: 9780979830105 (Paperback)
Library of Congress Control Number: 2007905556

First Revised Edition

www.facebook.com/savingonenationundergod

www.libertyaloud.com

libertyaloud@gmail.com

www.libraryanded.com
Library and Educational Services, LLC
Buchanan, MI 49107

Book design by Ken Raymond

This book is printed on acid-free paper.

Lovingly dedicated to
Ken,
Stephanie, Nicholas, Jurian, & Leander
Michael & Vicky,
Theresa, and Laura

and to my parents, John and Patsy,
two of the greatest from the "Greatest Generation"

CONTENTS

ONE

HOW IT BEGAN

In 1888, no one in America had ever seen a movie or a skyscraper. No one had ever ridden a Ferris Wheel or tasted a chocolate bar. There were thirty-eight states in the United States, Grover Cleveland was president, and the Statue of Liberty was two years old. The zipper had not yet been invented. Neither had basketball, Band-Aids, or corn flakes.

In 1888, no one had ever heard a commercial, a siren, a lawn mower ... or the Pledge of Allegiance.

But an advertisement in a popular children's magazine would spark a new idea, an idea that would eventually culminate in children all across America reciting the Pledge of Allegiance for the first time as part of a very special celebration.

This is the ad that ran in *The Youth's Companion* in 1888 and this is where the idea of the Pledge of Allegiance began.

You see, the ad was more than a pitch to sell flags. It was also a plea for parents, teachers, and communities to inspire patriotism in America's youth.

Like today, many parents in the 1880s were anxious about their children's futures. They worried that the American ideals they had enjoyed as youngsters would be lost before their own children reached adulthood.

There was good reason to be concerned.

For one thing, the landscape of America was changing. The family farms and small towns that once dotted America's countryside seemed to be vanishing.

In their place grew crowded, noisy cities overflowing with people.

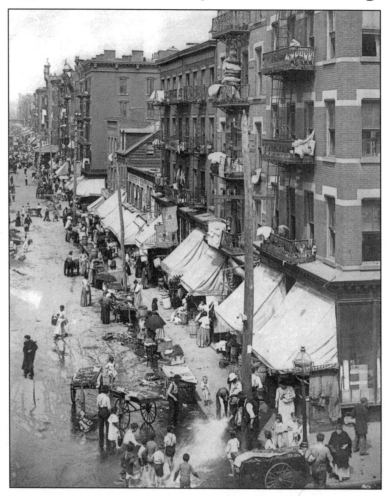

Drab tenement houses seemed to spring up from nowhere, bulging at the seams with masses of humanity. Strange machines occupied huge factories, mysteriously spitting out goods by the thousands that had formerly been handcrafted one at a time in homes.

Today we hardly blink an eye when we talk about this period of history known as the Industrial Revolution. But to the people who actually lived during this time, the change was often mind-boggling.

The face of America was also changing. Prior to the Civil War, relatively few people considered moving from their native country to live in America. But in the last half of the nineteenth century, that changed.

People from all corners of the world left their homeland by the millions to live in America, the land of liberty. Some came to escape war in their own country; others came to escape disease or famine. Many came simply to make better lives for themselves. Whatever their reasons, millions of immigrants came to live in the United States in the last half of the nineteenth century.

Most importantly, America's heart was changing. Even though the Civil War had ended, America remained a fractured nation—united on paper, but separated in spirit. You see, the Civil War had been so very bitter that it left the heart of America deeply wounded. Nearly every family had lost a father, brother, uncle, or son in the War. In all, *half a million Americans* died in that horrible war. Not surprisingly, the resentment between the North and the South continued to fester long after the War had ended.

America's unity was at stake. How could our nation survive with such bitter wounds?

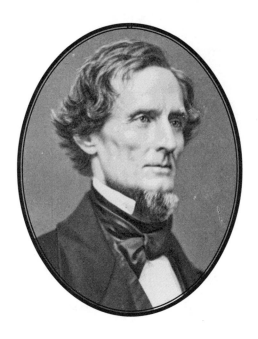

"In the next four years is ... locked up the fate of the Union."

~ Jefferson Davis,
President of the Confederate States of America

"A house divided against itself cannot stand."

~ Abraham Lincoln,
President of the United States of America

TWO
RAISE THE SCHOOLHOUSE FLAG

President Abraham Lincoln understood that the Civil War had indeed brought about a "new birth of freedom," but it had also cost America dearly. He knew how important it was for the nation's wounds to begin to heal.

Lincoln had begun planning a strategy to accomplish just that. He spoke very plainly to the nation of his plans in his second Inaugural Address on March 4, 1865:

> *"With malice toward none; with charity for all;*
> *with firmness in the right, as God gives us to see the right,*
> *let us strive on to finish the work we are in;*
> *to bind up the nation's wounds,*
> *to care for him who shall have borne the battle,*
> *and for his widow and his orphan –*
> *to do all which may achieve and cherish a just and lasting*
> *peace among ourselves, and with all nations."*

9

This photo was taken as President Lincoln delivered his second Inaugural Address. If you look along the lower railing in the photo, you will see a white pedestal. Abraham Lincoln is the tall man standing just behind it.

Tragically, President Lincoln was assassinated on April 15, 1865. His plan was never put into action. Such was the environment in America during the latter part of the 1800's.

That is why the advertisement that suggested the Stars and Stripes be flown in "homes and school-room" seemed like the right idea at the right time.

James Upham certainly thought so. After all, he created the "Schoolhouse Flag Movement." His goal was to place a flag in front of every public school in America.

Before Upham's campaign began, flags were scarce, flown only atop government buildings in large cities and military installations in remote locations. Some Americans might live their entire lives without ever seeing Old Glory. But, every community in the growing nation had a school, even if only a tiny one. A flag in front of the thousands of schools across the nation would remind all who passed of "the honor and glory of our native land."

James Bailey Upham

But, the flag campaign was only the first step of a much larger plan. Upham envisioned something much grander, something that had never before been attempted—the nation's schoolchildren simultaneously reciting a salute around the schoolhouse flag. The salute, yet to be composed, would be the feature of an event to take place in just a few years to celebrate one of America's most historic occasions.

But, before that could happen, James Upham had to find a way to place an American flag in front of thousands of schools across America.

Methodically, Upham began helping children acquire flags for their schools.

First, there was an essay contest.

Students across the nation were invited to compete by submitting a 600-word essay on the topic of "The Patriotic Influence of the American Flag." A winner from each state and territory was chosen. The prize, of course, was a new flag for the winner's school.

Each essay sent us must be accompanied by the name of the school, the author, and the town and State.

The school in each State sending us the best essay on the subject will receive from us, free of all expense, a Regulation Bunting Flag, nine by fifteen feet in size—**forty-two stars.**

The awards will be made as soon after April 1st as possible, in season for the schools to dedicate the Flags on the **Fourth of July, 1890.**

As soon as the award of Flags has been made THE YOUTH'S COMPANION will publish the names of the schools receiving them, also the names of the writers of the essays.

As a special bonus, *The Youth's Companion* promised to publish the names of the winners along with the names of the states, towns, and schools in the Fourth of July 1890 issue.

THE FLAG AND THE SCHOOL.

In January last *The Companion* offered as a prize to be competed for by the pupils in the public schools of each State and Territory, a United States flag. The flags, measuring nine feet by fifteen, and made of the best bunting, were to be awarded to that school in each State and Territory, one of whose pupils should submit the best essay, not exceeding six hundred words in length, upon the subject of "The Patriotic Influence of the American Flag when raised over the Public Schools."

Pupils in public schools of forty-one States and six Territories responded to this offer. The essays have been examined, the prizes awarded, and the flags sent and received; and many if not all of them have been raised over the school-houses. We give below a list of the schools and the essayists to whom the flags were awarded.

Can you imagine how exciting it must have been to these nineteenth-century youngsters to have their names published in a magazine mailed to hundreds of thousands of people throughout the nation? Look down the list—you may find your great-great-grandfather or great-great-grandmother's name!

THE FLAG-WINNERS.

MAINE, Skowhegan High School.
 May C. Parsons.
NEW HAMPSHIRE, South Merrimack School.
 Allie H. Harris.
VERMONT, Brandon Graded School.
 Asa W. Hawley.
MASSACHUSETTS, Upton High School.
 Anna L. Metcalf.
RHODE ISLAND, Olneyville High School.
 Walter R. Tourtellot.
CONNECTICUT, Norwich, Broadway School.
 Edith C. Flanders.
NEW YORK, N. Y. City, Tremont, Grammar School
 No. 63. Louis V. Fox.
NEW JERSEY, Warrenville Public School.
 Elizabeth G. Austin.
PENNSYLVANIA, Chester High School.
 Mary A. Martin.
DELAWARE, Smyrna Public School.
 Mary Budd.
MARYLAND, Simpsonville, School No. 4, District 5.
 Bettie Linthicum.
VIRGINIA, Bowers Hill, Jolliffs School.
 Oscar L. Peek.

WISCONSIN, West Bend High School.
 Roxy Knapp.
MINNESOTA, New Ulm Public School.
 Albert Pfaender.
NORTH DAKOTA, Grafton Public School.
 Henry B. Winne.
SOUTH DAKOTA, Vermillion Public School
 Mabel S. White.
COLORADO, Aspen High School.
 Frank Kinder.
NEVADA, Virginia City High School.
 Lillian White.
MONTANA, Sun River Public School, District No. 2.
 Charles A. Bull.
CALIFORNIA, Artesia Public School.
 Geo. Frampton, Jr.
OREGON, Damascus Public School, District No. 77.
 Myrtle Breithaupt.
WASHINGTON, Vancouver Public School.
 Walter Seward.
WYOMING, Rawlins Public School
 Edwin F. Bennett.
UTAH, Slaterville, New West School.
 Chas. M. Webb.
NEW MEXICO, Santa Fe Public School.
 Pedro R. Sandoval.
ARIZONA, Phoenix High School.
 Nellie Fowler.
IDAHO, Ceylon Public School, District 40
 Edwin Warenstaff.
INDIAN TER., Hennessey, Oklahoma, Pleasant View
 School. Ruth L. Coon.

WEST VIRGINIA, Wheeling, Webster Grammar School.
 Harry Creighton.
NORTH CAROLINA, Winston Public School.
 Fannie R. Coleman.
SOUTH CAROLINA, Darlington, Mayo School.
 Mabel L. Keith.
GEORGIA, Ben Hill, Ben Hill School.
 Lula Wood.
FLORIDA, Belleview Public School.
 Pearl Murdock.
ALABAMA, Tuscumbia School.
 Alice Denton.
MISSISSIPPI, Water Valley Public School.
 Minnie Markette.
TEXAS, Dallas, Central School.
 Daisy A. Holland.
TENNESSEE, Blountville Public School.
 Nannie V. Fain.
ARKANSAS, Eureka Springs School 7th Grade.
 James Brumfield.
KENTUCKY, Bowling Green Public School.
 Harry C. Temple.
OHIO, Coshocton High School.
 Mary D. James.
MICHIGAN, Mt. Pleasant High School.
 Maggie E. Richmond.
INDIANA, Logansport High School.
 Benj. F. Long.
ILLINOIS, Galesburg High School.
 Lizzie Hazzard.
MISSOURI, Springfield, Central School.
 Jetta Clay.
KANSAS, Clay Centre High School.
 Will L. Long.
IOWA, Oskaloosa High School.
 Bessie Johnson.
NEBRASKA, Lincoln High School.
 Flora Bullock.

Next, Upham created a plan that would help youngsters raise the money to buy a flag.

One hundred School Flag Certificates were sent—free—to any school child who mailed in a request. The certificates were really nothing more than a piece of paper. But the words on the paper made all the difference.

> **This Certificate**
>
> **Entitles the holder to a**
>
> **SHARE**
>
> **In the patriotic influences**
>
> **of the**
>
> **SCHOOL FLAG.**

Who could turn away such a request?

Week after week, hundreds of children mailed away to *The Youth's Companion* for a stack of certificates which were sold door-to-door to friends and neighbors. For a nickel, patrons quickly bought them all and another flag was soon on its way to Small Town, America.

Still not satisfied that every school in the nation had received a flag, Upham ran one final promotion.

This time, he offered teachers a beautifully illustrated poem to decorate their classrooms.   "Raising the Schoolhouse Flag" was written by Hezekiah Butterworth, a popular author and poet in the nineteenth century.

We have recently published a souvenir edition of THE YOUTH'S COMPANION'S illustrated Fourth of July Poem, entitled:

Raising the Schoolhouse Flag.

It is printed on heavy paper for **framing.**

We have already sent a copy to every public school that entered into the competition for THE YOUTH'S COMPANION Prize Flags.

We now offer to send FREE to all public schools in the United States that have already raised the United States Flag a copy of this Souvenir Picture.

In sending to us for this Souvenir the order must be signed either by the principal, or one of the teachers of the school. Address,

THE YOUTH'S COMPANION,
BOSTON, MASS.

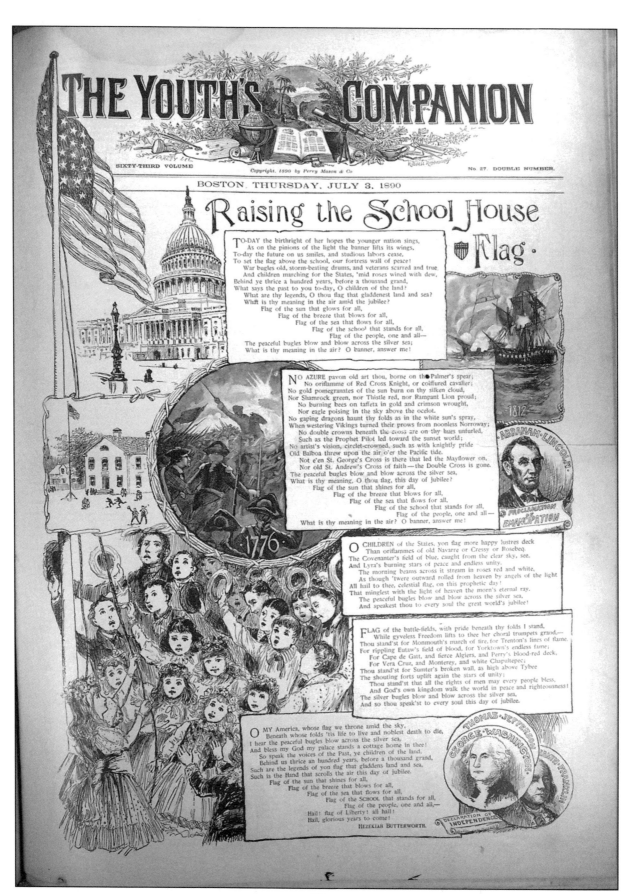

THE YOUTH'S COMPANION

SIXTY-THIRD VOLUME   Copyright, 1890 by Perry Mason & Co   No. 27. DOUBLE NUMBER.

BOSTON, THURSDAY, JULY 3, 1890

Raising the School House Flag.

TO-DAY the birthright of her hopes the younger nation sings,
    As on the pinions of the light the banner lifts its wings,
To-day the future on us smiles, and studious labors cease,
To set the flag above the school, our fortress wall of peace!
    War bugles old, storm-beating drums, and veterans scarred and true,
    And children marching for the States, 'mid roses wined with dew,
Behind ye thrice a hundred years, before a thousand grand,
What says the past to you to-day, O children of the land?
    What are thy legends, O thou flag that gladdenest land and sea?
    What is thy meaning in the air amid the jubilee?
        Flag of the sun that glows for all,
            Flag of the breeze that blows for all,
                Flag of the sea that flows for all,
                    Flag of the school that stands for all,
                        Flag of the people, one and all—
    The peaceful bugles blow and blow across the silver sea;
    What is thy meaning in the air? O banner, answer me!

NO AZURE pavon old art thou, borne on the Palmer's spear;
    No oriflamme of Red Cross Knight, or coiffured cavalier;
No gold pomegranates of the sun burn on thy silken cloud,
Nor Shamrock green, nor Thistle red, nor Rampant Lion proud;
    No burning bees on taffeta in gold and crimson wrought,
    Nor eagle poising in the sky above the ocelot.
No gaping dragons haunt thy folds as in the white sun's spray,
When westering Vikings turned their prows from noonless Norroway;
    No double crowns beneath the cross are on thy hues unfurled,
    Such as the Prophet Pilot led toward the sunset world;
No artist's vision, circlet-crowned, such as with knightly pride
Old Balboa threw upon the air o'er the Pacific tide.
    Not e'en St. George's Cross is there that led the Mayflower on,
    Nor old St. Andrew's Cross of faith—the Double Cross is gone.
The peaceful bugles blow and blow across the silver sea,
What is thy meaning, O thou flag, this day of jubilee?
    Flag of the sun that shines for all,
        Flag of the breeze that blows for all,
            Flag of the sea that flows for all,
                Flag of the school that stands for all,
                    Flag of the people, one and all—
    What is thy meaning in the air? O banner, answer me!

O CHILDREN of the States, yon flag more happy lustres deck
    Than oriflammes of old Navarre or Cressy or Rosebeq.
The Covenanter's field of blue, caught from the clear sky, see,
And Lyra's burning stars of peace and endless unity.
    The morning beams across it stream in roses red and white,
    As though 'twere outward rolled from heaven by angels of the light.
All hail to thee, celestial flag, on this prophetic day!
That minglest with the light of heaven the morn's eternal ray.
    The peaceful bugles blow and blow across the silver sea,
    And speakest thou to every soul the great world's jubilee!

FLAG of the battle-fields, with pride beneath thy folds I stand,
    While gyveless Freedom lifts to thee her choral trumpets grand,—
Thou stand'st for Monmouth's march of fire, for Trenton's lines of flame.
For rippling Eutaw's field of blood, for Yorktown's endless fame;
    For Cape de Gatt, and fierce Algiers, and Perry's blood-red deck,
    For Vera Cruz, and Monterey, and white Chapultepec;
Thou stand'st for Sumter's broken wall, as high above Tybee
The shouting forts uplift again the stars of unity!
    Thou stand'st that all the rights of men may every people bless,
    And God's own kingdom walk the world in peace and righteousness!
The silver bugles blow and blow across the silver sea,
And so thou speak'st to every soul this day of jubilee.

O MY America, whose flag we throne amid the sky,
    Beneath whose folds 'tis life to live and noblest death to die,
I hear the peaceful bugles blow across the silver sea,
And bless my God my palace stands a cottage home in thee!
    So speak the voices of the Past, ye children of the land,
    Behind us thrice an hundred years, before a thousand grand,
Such are the legends of yon flag that gladdens land and sea,
Such is the Hand that scrolls the air this day of jubilee.
    Flag of the sun that shines for all,
        Flag of the breeze that blows for all,
            Flag of the sea that flows for all,
                Flag of the SCHOOL that stands for all,
                    Flag of the people, one and all,—
    Hail! flag of Liberty! all hail!
    Hail, glorious years to come!

HEZEKIAH BUTTERWORTH.

As more and more schools flew the Stars and Stripes in their yards, students and teachers began to create simple patriotic programs to accompany the raising of the flag each morning. The growing trend was addressed in an article entitled, "The School Flag." Following is an excerpt from that article:

"The boys are moving in the matter of raising the flag of the United States over the school-houses on national and festive days. The girls are helping them with sympathy and subscriptions. ... We suggest also that a little, not too much, ceremony in the raising and lowering of the flag will add to the impressiveness of the occasion."

We send with each Flag appropriate Flag Exercises for a public raising.

The recitation of a patriotic pledge was particularly encouraged in New York City schools, where the number of immigrant children greatly outnumbered children who were born in the United States.

As early as 1880, "The American Patriotic Salute" was a traditional part of every New York City student's early education. Written by George Balch, it was one of many citizenship lessons included in *The Patriotic Primer for Little Citizens* and was recited each morning before classes began. Standing at attention, with the flag held in front of the classroom, the students would first touch their foreheads, then their hearts, while reciting in unison:

"We give our heads! And our hearts! to God! And our country!"

Next, with their right arms outstretched toward the flag, they exclaimed, *"One Country! One Language! One Flag!"*

As each month passed, more and more schools ordered flags.

The Flag
AND THE
Public Schools

THE YOUTH'S COMPANION, in one of its issues of more than a year ago, set forth the idea of the Flag and the Public Schools.

The idea is becoming popular, and the American Flag can now be seen floating over many a patriotic school.

Raising the School House Flag.

We have just printed a new edition, in two tints, of the beautiful Illustrated Souvenir Poem, "Raising the School House Flag."

Has your school raised a flag?

If so, you are entitled to the Souvenir. Let your teacher sign the order, and we will send it to your school free, postage paid by us.

If your school has *not* yet raised a flag and yet wishes to, let us know it and we will mail you **free one hundred School Flag Certificates.** With these Certificates scores of schools have raised money for a $10 flag in one day's time. If you wish the Certificates one of the teachers must sign the order.

THE YOUTH'S COMPANION, Boston, Mass.

Flags for Our Public Schools.

In 1888 THE YOUTH'S COMPANION inaugurated the general Public Schoolhouse Flag movement.

Since that time the raising of the Flag over the Public School has become a National custom.

Could the Stars and Stripes be hung upon the the walls of every home, and float over every public school in the land, how grandly might patriotism and love of liberty be unceasingly taught.

In many localities it is difficult to obtain good Flags. We have arranged to supply the best quality of Flags at very low prices.

United States Bunting Flag. Regulation sizes.

6 x 4 ft. $3.30.   Given for two subscribers and $1.80 additional.
9 x 6 ft.   5.00.   Given for four subscribers and $2.25 additional.
12 x 7½ ft.   6.60.   Given for six subscribers and $2.60 additional.
20 x 10 ft.   13.00.   Given for ten subscribers and $6.00 additional.

All the Flags have 44 stars. With the two largest Flags we will include a Canvas Bag for keeping the Flag when not in use. We will also letter this Bag free—after this arrangement: "Lincoln School—Presented by Henry Smith." **They must be sent by express and charges paid by receiver,** when sent as a premium or purchased.

THE FLAG
and the Public Schools.

To save correspondence we publish the following:

MINNEAPOLIS, MINN., Oct. 10, '90. MESSRS. PERRY MASON & CO.— *Gentlemen:* In your issue of THE YOUTH'S COMPANION of Oct. 9th you offered to send free to any public school that had already raised the U. S. Flag, a copy of the Souvenir edition of the illustrated poem, "Raising the School House Flag." Since that date our school has raised a beautiful flag. We also very much wish the Souvenir to frame and hang in our school-room. May we be allowed to share in the offer you so generously made?

Yours very truly,   ——— ———.

TO SUCH WE REPLY: To all public schools that have raised a flag, and to all schools that **may do so in the future,** we will send **free** a copy of the Souvenir. All applications for these Souvenirs must be signed either by the principal or one of the teachers of the school.   THE YOUTH'S COMPANION, Boston, Mass.

Before long, American flags surrounded by saluting children

became a common scene each morning at schools across the nation.

THREE

THE COLUMBIAN
PUBLIC SCHOOL CELEBRATION

By 1890 *The Youth's Companion* reached the homes of more than one-half million Americans each week. Owner and editor Daniel Ford set high standards in literary quality and moral character that not only grew the weekly into one of the most popular of its day but also helped shape the hearts and minds of its many young readers.

Mark Twain, Emily Dickinson, Jack London, Theodore Roosevelt, and Winston Churchill were among those whose articles and stories were published during the life of *The Youth's Companion.* One *Companion* reader became a well-known author herself. In her book, *The Long Winter,* Laura Ingalls Wilder memorialized *The Youth's Companion* by describing how it helped her cope with the hardships of the deadly 1888 blizzard.

In an age when children had few toys or amusements, the Christmas edition of *The Youth's Companion* was eagerly anticipated.

Maybe that's why Upham chose to reveal the first glimpse of his extraordinary plan on December 25, 1890.

Among advertisements for products such as Ayer's sarsaparilla, Bailey's rubber heel cushions and Beecham's Pills (painless and effectual for bilious and nervous disorders), the familiar flag ad caught the eye of its young readers.

But, this ad was different.

As a matter of fact, it was not an ad at all. It was an invitation.

Schools were encouraged to commemorate the 400th anniversary of Christopher Columbus's discovery of America by participating in the Columbus Public School Celebration. On October 12, 1892, there was to be a national party like no other seen before.

Is your School to Celebrate?

ASK YOUR Teacher to decide about the Celebration at once and drop us a letter or postal **next week**. We wish to know. In due time the Chairman of the Executive Committee on the Celebration will send your school the **Official Programme** to be used at your Celebration on the 12th of October. Did you know that 13,000,000 school children are to unite in this

Columbian Public School Celebration?

Let us also know it if you have no Flag for your School House. We will, if requested, send you **free** 100 "Flag Certificates." These will enable you to raise the money for a Flag within two days. Thousands of Schools have done this. Get your Flag and thus be ready for the National Columbian Public School Celebration. Get the Flag now and raise it for the first time on the Fourth of July.

Don't let your school be left out. Every Public School House in America ought to raise its Flag on Columbus Day and beneath its folds join in the National celebration. Ask your teacher to write us at once.

The Youth's Companion,
BOSTON, MASS.

The youth of America were all invited, and the new flags would represent the Guest of Honor!

Of course, James Upham was not the only person in America who had been thinking about the upcoming anniversary. No, this was an occasion so momentous . . . so meaningful . . . so historic that national leaders had spent the previous ten years discussing ways to celebrate it, but nothing ever seemed to get off the ground.

One idea, however, came up again and again, and finally, in the waning days of 1890 there was a second celebration in the making.

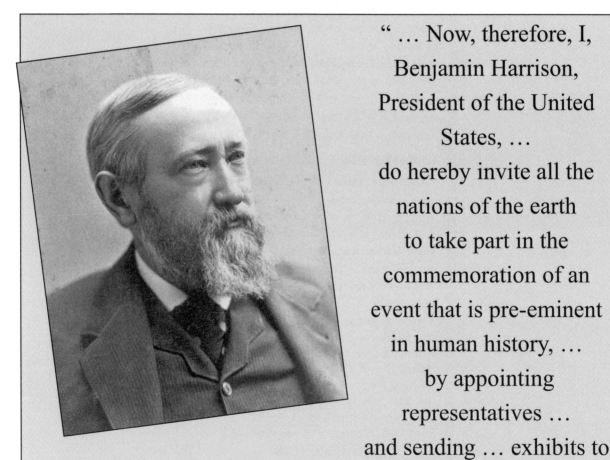

" … Now, therefore, I, Benjamin Harrison, President of the United States, …
do hereby invite all the nations of the earth
to take part in the commemoration of an event that is pre-eminent in human history, …
by appointing representatives …
and sending … exhibits to the World's Columbian Exposition …"

America now had not one but two ways to celebrate the historic anniversary—the World's Columbian Exposition and the National Public School Celebration.

The Exposition was scheduled to open on the 400th anniversary of Columbus's discovery and close a year later. People from all over the world made plans to travel to Chicago, the host city, eager to experience the sights and sounds of the world's newest inventions, discoveries, and breakthroughs.

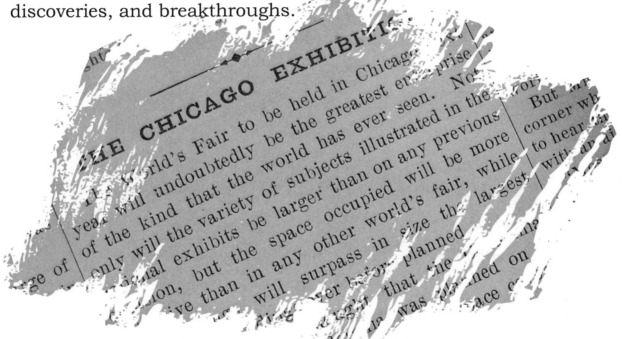

THE CHICAGO EXHIBITI...

...World's Fair to be held in Chicago...year...will undoubtedly be the greatest enterprise...of the kind that the world has ever seen. Not...only will the variety of subjects illustrated in the...exhibits be larger than on any previous...on, but the space occupied will be more...ve than in any other world's fair, while...will surpass in size the largest...planned...that the...was planned on...

But not every American could travel to Chicago. And certainly all of America could not crowd into Chicago on the day of the celebration. Every American could, however, attend a local celebration at their town school.

This was the beauty of Upham's plan: It allowed all of America to celebrate at the same time and in the same way—one huge, national family celebrating its discovery together.

No one was more excited about the National Public School Celebration than James Upham, who began working harder than ever to see his dream become a reality. Immediately he began planning what would become one of the most memorable events of the nineteenth century.

It wasn't long, however, before the demands of planning an event of such mammoth proportions began to overwhelm the newspaper's small staff.

Fortunately, Daniel Ford had hired an assistant for Upham, a young Baptist preacher who had recently left the pulpit to develop his writing talents. The young man's name was Francis Bellamy. He and Upham quickly became friends, forging a powerful working relationship that continued for many years. The two men found that their talents complemented one another—Upham mastering the overall vision of the celebration and Bellamy carrying out the details.

With interest in the Public School Celebration growing rapidly, Ford wasted no time assigning Bellamy as chairman of the Executive Committee of the National Public School Celebration.

As Bellamy thrust himself into his work, he noticed that a very important detail had been overlooked—a detail that, if left unattended, could mean the difference between the success and failure of the entire project.

The date of the celebration, October 12, had not been declared a national holiday. Without such a declaration, there was a good chance it would pass completely unnoticed in some areas of the country.

Francis Bellamy

Such an action required a resolution from the United States Congress—with the President's signature, no less!

And so, Bellamy, with just a few months before the actual event was to take place, packed his bags and made his way to Washington, D.C. He had to speak to the President!

35

FOUR

BE IT RESOLVED

It was early May 1892 when Francis Bellamy and his wife, Hattie, arrived at the Hotel Oxford in Washington, D.C.

Bellamy had one goal in mind—to persuade President Benjamin Harrison to issue a proclamation declaring Columbus Day a national holiday and allowing the schools to lead the celebration.

The trip was a whirlwind of activity for Bellamy. Interviews, meetings, and conferences filled the hours of each day, as he went from one congressional office to another. The sentiment was nearly unanimous for Bellamy's recommendation to make October 12 a national holiday.

Although Bellamy had to return to Boston before the final vote was taken, by the end of his trip he felt certain that he had accomplished his mission and that Congress would pass the resolution.

It wasn't long after returning home that Bellamy received the answer he hoped for.

May 23rd 1892

Francis Bellamy, Esq.
    Chairman, &c

My dear Sir:

    I have your letter of May 12th in which you bring before me the proposition which has had some discussion in the public press, to observe the 400th Anniversary of the Discovery of America, by demonstrations in the public schools. I am very much pleased with the idea. Properly conducted such exercises will be very instructive to the pupils, and will excite in every village in the land an interest in this great anniversary.

    Very truly yours,

    Benj. Harrison

With the assurance of the President's support, Bellamy was elated when he read in the morning papers of June 21 that Congress had approved the resolution. The anniversary would indeed be a national holiday.

But his heart sank when he saw the date that Congress had named as the holiday. Instead of October 12, the resolution read October *21*!

Now, therefore, I, Benjamin Harrison, President of the United States of America, . . . do hereby appoint Friday, October 21, 1892, the four hundredth anniversary of the Discovery of America by Columbus, as a general holiday for the people of the United States. On that day let the people, so far as possible, cease from toil and devote themselves to such exercises as may best express honor to the Discoverer and their appreciation of the great achievements of the four completed centuries of American life.

Columbus stood in his age as the pioneer of progress and enlightenment. The system of universal education is in our age the most prominent and salutary feature of the spirit of enlightenment, and it is peculiarly appropriate that the schools be made by the people the center of the day's demonstration. Let the National Flag float over every school house in the country, and the exercises be such as shall impress upon our youth the patriotic duties of American citizenship.

In the churches and in the other places of assembly of the people, let there be expressions of gratitude to Divine Providence for the devout faith of the Discoverer, and for the Divine care and guidance which has directed our history and so abundantly blessed our people. . . ."

This ad ran on June 2nd—just days before Bellamy was notified that Congress had approved October 21st as the date of the celebration. Notice that it gives the "12th of October, 1892" as the date of the celebration.

Imagine Francis Bellamy, a young man starting a new career, having been promoted to a very important position, having just returned from meeting the President of the United States and discussing plans for a once-in-a-lifetime event commemorating the most historic occasion of the century. He would have only a few short months to complete the plans and communicate them to every city, town, and village in America! And then he realized that the entire nation had been invited to celebrate the anniversary on the *wrong date*!

In fact, the mistake was not a misunderstanding, nor was it a typographical error. The correct date for the celebration *was* indeed October 21, not October 12!

To understand how the discrepancy occurred requires both a history and a math lesson.

In 1492, when Christopher Columbus discovered the New World, he used the Julian calendar, which was used by all civilized people at that time. But in 1582, ninety years after Columbus's discovery, the Julian calendar was replaced by the Gregorian calendar. In the process of switching the two, corrections were made to make the new calendar more accurate.

THE YOUTH'S COMPANION

1492

NEW YEAR'S NUMBER

THE COLUMBIAN YEAR

1892

One day was eliminated for each decade. In this case, nine days were eliminated—which meant the October 12 date was really nine days ahead of the actual date of Columbus's landing.

Bellamy had no other choice but to advertise the new date.

With no explanation as to why the date was changed, *The Youth's Companion* ran this ad less than a month before the celebration.

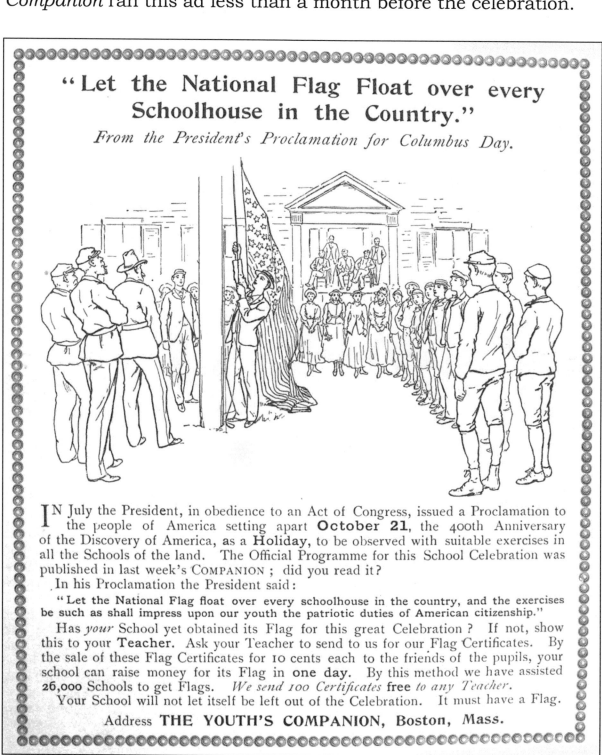

Public School Celebration,

October 21, 1892.

"Let the National Flag Float over every Schoolhouse in the Country."

From the President's Proclamation for Columbus Day.

HAS YOUR SCHOOL A FLAG?

If not, show this to your Teacher.   Ask her to send to us for our Flag Certificates. By the sale of these Flag Certificates for 10 cents each to the friends of the pupils, your school can raise money for its Flag in one day.   By this method we have assisted **26,000** Schools to get Flags.   *We send 100 Certificates* **free** *to any teacher.*

Address THE YOUTH'S COMPANION,   **Boston, Mass.**

FIVE

The Pledge Makes Its Debut

Now that the School Celebration was officially declared a national holiday, the two editors focused their attention on creating an inspiring program for the nation's schools to follow. Their goal was to recognize the grandeur of the occasion while expressing the simple but profound truths that made America great.

Bellamy and Upham held uppermost in their minds that the celebration was for *all* America, from the largest school in the biggest city to the smallest school in the tiniest village.

Both men knew the new flags had to be at center stage of the event. To best accomplish this, a vow or pledge to the flag was needed.

According to historical records, the men discussed their ideas over and over. But struggle as they might, neither could pen the words that appropriately expressed the meaning of the moment.

Time was drawing near.

This photo of Francis Bellamy is believed to have been taken in 1900.

By late August, with the Public School Celebration a little over a month away, the final touches were added to the Official Programme. But the task of writing a salute for the flag still remained. As a matter of fact, the first word had not yet been written!

Just two weeks remained to meet the deadline to publish the school program in time for schools to begin rehearsing.

By this time, thousands of schools had new American flags flying in their school yards while teachers and pupils waited in anticipation for instructions from *The Youth's Companion*.

DISTRICT NO. 9, FROM A PHOTOGRAPH.

Raise the Schoolhouse Flag.

The patriotic and plucky schoolmistress of District No. 9, Clark township, Ind., raised the American flag over her schoolhouse.

The day after it was raised the flagstaff was cut down, the flag torn from its guys and spirited away.

"I shall procure a new flagstaff and raise another flag next Monday if I have to do it myself, and it shall stay there, too." She not only raised the new flagstaff and flag, but she got a Winchester rifle, with which to defend it if need be.

The flag still waves over the little schoolhouse of District No. 9. Later the citizens of Crawfordsville, Ind., presented her a beautiful silk flag in honor of her patriotic devotion to her country's flag.

Over and over the fatigued editors had discussed writing a salute, a vow, or a promise. The significance of the moment was as clear to them as the deadline they faced. They tossed around one idea after another, but nothing seemed to work. They discussed using one of the many different salutes in use at the time. But they both agreed that nothing already in existence seemed to embody the sense of history required for so great an occasion.

Now we must stop for a moment to think about something. At that moment in history, no one dreamed that the chosen salute would become the Pledge of Allegiance, which is as familiar to us as our own names, or that it would eventually become a precious tradition in American life.

Bellamy and Upham were not trying to write a historic vow or pledge. They were simply trying to do the very best job they could for a very important event. If the truth be known, most of their energy was likely focused on the pomp and circumstance of the occasion.

And that is why the salute, as critical as it was to the overall program, was left as the last item to complete.

As the story goes, when procrastination was no longer an option, Upham urged Bellamy to lock himself in his office and, at the very least, draft an outline. The story continues that hours later, Bellamy emerged with the Pledge of Allegiance scribbled on a scrap of paper.

Have you noticed that there is no signature beneath the handwritten Pledge? Because it is unsigned, the true author of the Pledge of Allegiance will forever remain a mystery.

Experts have gathered many times to decide once and for all the answer to the Pledge's authorship. The only possibilities were Francis Bellamy and James Upham. But because neither man realized in 1892 that the Pledge would become what we know it as today—a time-honored and much-loved American tradition—and because Daniel Ford insisted that his editors' articles remain anonymous—neither man bothered to claim authorship at the time of its writing.

Many years passed before people began to wonder who had composed the Pledge. By that time, James Upham had died, taking to his grave any memory of his part in its composition. Although Upham's relatives insisted that it was he who had composed the Pledge, they could not produce the evidence to prove it. Bellamy, on the other hand, had kept the scrap of paper and could prove the handwriting to be his.

The critical question that can never be answered remains: Did Bellamy actually compose the Pledge or did he simply write it down as Upham dictated it aloud to him?

Only those two men know exactly what transpired in the offices of *The Youth's Companion* that warm August evening so long ago.

Both Bellamy and Upham agreed that what was written could not be improved upon in any way. It was simple enough for youngsters to memorize, yet it perfectly captured the true spirit of America.

446 ·   THE YOUTH'S COMPANION.   SEPTEMBER 8, 1892.

National School Celebration of Columbus Day.

THE OFFICIAL PROGRAMME.

Let every pupil and friend of the Schools who reads THE COMPANION, at once present personally the following programme to the Teachers, Superintendents, School Boards, and Newspapers in the towns and cities in which they reside. Not one School in America should be left out in this Celebration.

After months of anticipation, the Official Programme finally appeared to readers on September 8, 1892. Now schools and town officials could begin to make their preparations.

Imagine the excitement felt throughout the nation as the new holiday approached! Mothers sewed special costumes, teachers organized Color Guards, mayors planned parade routes, and town bands began practicing patriotic music.

Children huddled together during lunch and after school. Haltingly at first, no doubt stumbling over the strange and unfamiliar words, the first generation of American children to recite the Pledge of Allegiance began to rehearse the words: "I pledge allegiance . . ."

It was here in the Official Programme that the Pledge of Allegiance made its public debut.

1. READING OF THE PRESIDENT'S PROCLAMATION,
   by the Master of Ceremonies.

   At the close of the reading he announces: "In accordance with this recommendation by the Pres[ident of the United] States, and as a sign of our devotion [to our flag] the Flag of the Nation be unfurled abo[ve us]

2. RAISING OF THE FLAG,

   As the Flag reaches the top of the sta[ff, the pupils] lead the assemblage in "Three Cheers [for the Flag."]

3. SALUTE TO THE FLAG,   *by the Pupils.*

   At a signal from the Principal the pupils, in ordered ranks, hands to the side, face the Flag. Another signal is given; every pupil gives the Flag the military salute—right hand lifted, palm downward, to a line with the forehead and close to it. Standing thus, all repeat together, slowly: "I pledge allegiance to my Flag and the Republic for which it stands: one Nation indivisible, with Liberty and Justice for all." At the words, "to my Flag," the right hand is extended gracefully, palm upward, towards the Flag, and remains in this gesture till the end of the affirmation; whereupon all hands immediately drop to the side. Then, still standing, as the instruments strike a chord, all will sing AMERICA—"My Country, 'tis of Thee."

4. ACKNOWLEDGMENT OF GOD.   Prayer or Scripture.

5. SONG OF COLUMBUS DAY, *by Pupils and Audience.*
   Contributed by The Youth's Companion.
   Air: Lyons.

   Columbia, my land! all hail the glad day
   When first to thy strand Hope pointed the way;
   Hail him who thro' darkness first followed the Flame
   That led where the Mayflower of Liberty came.

   Dear Country, the star of the valiant and free!
   Thy exiles afar are dreaming of thee.
   No fields of the Earth so enchantingly shine,
   No air breathes such incense, such music as thine.

   Humanity's home! thy sheltering breast
   Gives welcome and room to strangers oppress'd.

54

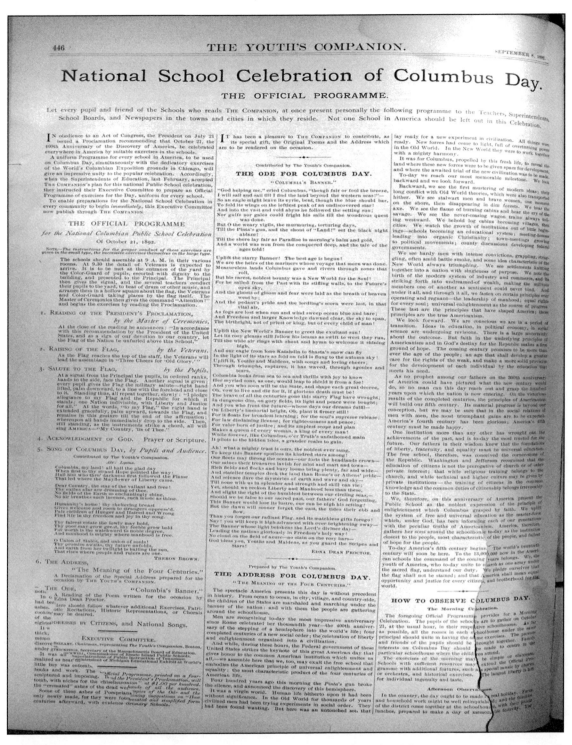

The Official Programme took up two-and-a-half pages. It included long speeches, flowery poems, and important salutations. But only the simple twenty-two-word Pledge of Allegiance is still remembered today.

SIX

COLUMBUS DAY, 1892

On Friday, October 21, 1892, every city and town across America buzzed with holiday excitement. Newspaper accounts described the events.

In Brooklyn, New York, half a million people gathered to watch a spectacular parade that lasted four hours and included twenty-five thousand marchers. In Newark, New Jersey, five thousand school children waved flags as they paraded alongside their neighbors of Italian descent. In San Francisco, California, "all the churches were largely attended" and San Franciscans later gathered at the schools to watch the presentation of the flag. In Trenton, New Jersey, the "largest parade ever seen in this city occurred . . . when the Hungarian, Irish, Spanish, and French societies, together with the Grand Army of the Republic and Sons of Veterans celebrated Columbus Day." In Boston, Massachusetts, "the principal of each school read to his scholars . . . the 145 Psalm; this was followed by the reading of the President's proclamation . . . next came the exercise of saluting the flag . . . *America*, Dr. S.F. Smith's famous hymn, was then sung by pupils and audience."

No matter how the celebrations differed from city to city, the one exercise common to all was the recitation of the Pledge around the schoolhouse flag.

This parade took place in Chicago, Illinois, on October 21, 1892, as part of the Dedication Day ceremony for the World's Columbian Exposition.

Originally, plans were made to open the World's Fair on October 21, 1892. But the organizers soon realized that the 1892 deadline was too optimistic and so, it was decided to dedicate the Fair buildings in October and then wait to officially open the Fair the following year. As it turned out, the Dedication Day celebration was every bit as grand as the opening. Here is how *The Chicago Daily Tribune* described it: "ARMY OF CHILDREN ... Ten Thousand March in Honor of Columbus ... MAKE A SPENDID ARRAY ... Fifth Avenue a Scene of Brilliancy and Grandeur ... CATHOLICS OUT IN FORCE ... Vice-President Morton and Governor Flower Loudly Cheered ... FLAGSTAFFS ON THE CHURCHES."

Here is how the National Public School Columbian Celebration looked in New York City.

In 1892, photographs were not published in newspapers, but following are some of the headlines describing the Columbus Day events in *The New York Times*.

"YOUNG AMERICA LEADS OFF ... FIRST OF THE GREAT PARADES OF COLUMBUS WEEK ... Almost 25,000 School Children and College Boys March Before Hundreds of Thousands"

And another description:

"THE OLD WORLD'S FESTIVAL ... SPAIN'S CELEBRATION OF THE GREAT DISCOVERY ... A BIG MEDIEVAL PARADE IN MADRID"

In Washington, D.C., the environment was anything but festive—President Benjamin Harrison's wife, Carolyn, lay dying in the White House. "The President and all the occupants of the White House were very much depressed in spirit this morning at the sudden change for the worse in Mrs. Harrison's condition."

In a separate article, *The New York Times* reported that, in Washington, D.C., "the discovery of America celebrated in the churches and schools, but there was no elaborate observance of the day."

Carolyn Harrison died on October 25, 1892.

One *New York Times* journalist summed it up best: "It is apparent from telegraphic dispatches that Columbus Day was observed in cities, towns and villages throughout the whole country with the greatest enthusiasm. School children paraded everywhere and religious services were well attended."

It is estimated that the Pledge of Allegiance was spoken in public for the first time by twelve million school children on that cool autumn day so long ago.

James Upham's dream had come true. Americans had, indeed, united under the banner of freedom, ready to step into a century that would test the character of an ever-growing nation.

SEVEN

"ONE NATION, UNDER GOD"

Time passed and America grew, taking on new challenges and adventures. Naturally, the growth brought with it changes to our thriving nation—changes that are reflected in the Pledge.

The first change came in 1923, when national leaders gathered for the first time to write a uniform set of guidelines on how to handle the United States flag properly.

Camp-Fire Girls saluting the Flag

In the beginning years of the twentieth century, America fought and won World War I. Patriotism was once again energized, and flag waving grew in popularity. By this time, nearly every state and dozens of patriotic organizations had written individual guidelines on the how to handle the flag.

Each guide book had different rules. One book instructed raising the flag one way; another book instructed something altogether different. And salutes were different from school to school, region to region, and state to state. The "raised arm" salute was still popular, although in some regions the palm was turned upward and in other regions it was turned downward. To add to the confusion, children in some states saluted the flag with a military salute either at the forehead or at their heart. The result was a confusing mish-mash of rules that differed from place to place.

In 1923, the American Legion gathered all of the patriotic organizations in the country to decide once and for all which set of rules would govern America's patriotic traditions. The rules they agreed upon would make up *The Flag Code*, a booklet that would be distributed throughout the country.

President Warren Harding was invited to open the meeting. In his remarks, he asked that the "Star Spangled Banner" be adopted as the national anthem. At that time, Americans sang a variety of songs at patriotic events, but there was no official national anthem.

As the meeting progressed, a lady—we know her only as Mrs. Weyman—stood up to say something about the Pledge of Allegiance. "Mr. Chairman, at present we pledge allegiance to 'my flag.' I would suggest we change that and say, 'I pledge allegiance to the United States flag'," she urged.

Mrs. Weyman's idea rang true. Indeed, Americans knew that millions of children would recite the Pledge of Allegiance and that many of them would likely be newly arriving immigrant children. Pledging loyalty to the flag "of the United States" would help them become good American citizens. And so, in 1923, the Pledge of Allegiance was changed for the first time. The following year, the words, "of America," were added.

The participants also discussed how the flag would be saluted. The "raised arm" salute was still popular, and so it was among the salutes included in *The Flag Code.* At this time in history, there were no bad feelings associated with the "raised arm" salute.

But, in the 1930's, an evil regime arose in Germany. It was called the Nazi regime, led by Adolph Hitler. Hitler murdered many millions of innocent people, both in Germany and in other countries. His goal was to take over the world. Nazis used the raised arm salute to pledge their loyalty to Hitler. America went to war to stop him. That terrible war was called World War II.

After many years of fighting, America won World War II and the raised arm salute was replaced by the hand-over-the-heart salute.

In 1942, fifty years after it was written, the Pledge of Allegiance became federal law and the hand-over-heart salute became its official salute. Gridley Adams, one of the leaders who helped write *The Flag Code,* explained, "After all, the Pledge of Allegiance is decidedly more a matter of the heart than of the muscle."

After fighting two World Wars to defeat enemies that threatened America's way of life, the Pledge of Allegiance had become a much beloved and important patriotic tradition.

> *I pledge allegiance*
> *to the flag*
> *of the United States*
> *of America*
> *and to the republic*
> *for which it stands*
> *one nation,*
> *indivisible,*
> *with liberty and justice for all.*

During the mid-twentieth century, America's future was again threatened—this time by a worldwide takeover of Communism.

Communism is a form of government that is distinctly unlike America's republican form of government. The most basic difference concerns the way the two governments acknowledge God.

Communism denies the existence of God and, therefore, denies its citizens the right to express their belief in God.

On the other hand, America was begun as a nation that recognizes God's existence and therefore allows its citizens the freedom to express their belief in God however they wish. The Declaration of Independence states, "We hold these truths to be self-evident, that all men are created equal, endowed by their Creator with certain unalienable Rights, that among these are life, liberty and the pursuit of happiness." In other words, the United States government is based on the belief that freedom comes from God, the "Creator."

National leaders recognized this stark difference between America and Communism and saw the Pledge of Allegiance as an opportunity to daily remind Americans of our dependence on God.

On February 8, 1954, two Congressmen from Michigan, Representative Louis C. Rabaut and Senator Homer Ferguson, proposed inserting the phrase "under God" to Congress. The date was chosen because it was the fifth anniversary of the imprisonment of a Hungarian Catholic, Cardinal Joseph Mindszenty. Cardinal Mindszenty had been arrested, tortured, and imprisoned by the Communists because he refused to stop warning his countrymen that Communism was dangerous.

Americans were aghast that a government would treat one of its citizens so unjustly simply because of his belief in God. They wanted to make a statement to the world that it is precisely because of God that people have freedom in the first place. Newspapers began running editorials supporting the addition of "under God" to the Pledge. People in many states recited it with the phrase, even before a Resolution was passed by Congress.

As Congressman Rabaut spoke before Congress, he stated, " 'Under God' in the Pledge of Allegiance to the flag expresses, aptly and forcefully, a grateful nation's attitude of dependence upon Almighty God. . . . For under God this Nation lives. . . . Indeed, the one fundamental issue which is the unbridgeable gap between America and Communist Russia is belief in Almighty God."

Senator Ferguson asserted that the addition of the phrase "under God" would " . . . acclaim to the Communists who deny the existence of God that the United States lives under His guidance."

Just the day before, President Dwight Eisenhower attended church, where he heard a sermon preached by Rev. George McPherson Docherty. In his sermon, Rev. Docherty proposed that there was something missing from the Pledge of Allegiance. That "something" was the mention of God. It was this sermon that convinced the President to sign the bill when it came to his desk.

The basis of Rev. Docherty's sermon was America's dependence on God, as expressed in the Gettysburg Address, a speech delivered by Abraham Lincoln at a ceremony to dedicate a cemetery of fallen Civil War soldiers. It is one of America's most famous and beloved speeches. In it, the phrase, "nation, under God," was used for the first time.

" ... The world will little note, nor long remember what we say here, but it can never forget what they did here. It is for us the living, rather, to be dedicated here to the unfinished work which they who fought here have thus far so nobly advanced. It is rather for us to be here dedicated to the great task remaining before us—that from these honored dead we take increased devotion to that cause for which they gave the last full measure of devotion—that we here highly resolve that these dead shall not have died in vain—that this nation, under God, shall have a new birth of freedom—and that government of the people, by the people, for the people, shall not perish from the earth."

Early in 1954 Congress voted unanimously to pass a resolution adopting the change. The ceremony enacting the revised Pledge of Allegiance took place, appropriately, on Flag Day, June 14, 1954.

This photo shows the Pledge of Allegiance being recited with the phrase, "under God," for the first time.

From left to right, the Congressional leaders are: U.S. Senators Styles Bridges, William F. Knowland, Lyndon B. Johnson, and Earle C. Clements, Congressmen Louis C. Rabaut, and Leslie C. Arends, Senator Homer Ferguson, and Congressman Sid Simpson.

President Dwight D. Eisenhower issued the following statement when he signed this bill into law:

"From this day forward, the millions of our school children will daily proclaim in every city and town, every village and rural school house, the dedication of our nation and our people to the Almighty.

To anyone who truly loves America, nothing could be more inspiring than to contemplate this rededication of our youth, on each school morning, to our country's true meaning.

Especially is this meaningful as we regard today's world. Over the globe, mankind has been cruelly torn by violence and brutality and, by the millions, deadened in mind and soul by a materialistic philosophy of life. Man everywhere is appalled by the prospect of atomic war.

In this somber setting, this law and its effects today have profound meaning. In this way we are reaffirming the transcendence of religious faith in America's heritage and future; in this way we shall constantly strengthen those spiritual weapons which forever will be our country's most powerful resource, in peace or in war."

...Under God

I pledge allegiance
to the flag
of the United States
of America
and to the Republic
for which it stands,
one Nation *under God*,
indivisible, with liberty
and justice for all.

For over one hundred years, Americans have proudly recited the Pledge of Allegiance. We learn it in school as soon as we learn the ABCs and although we don't understand the strange words at first, as we grow older, we begin to understand their meaning. James Upham and Francis Bellamy hoped that, by repeating the words over and over again, each generation of Americans would not only inherit a nation where liberty flourishes and justice abounds, but will also dedicate themselves to passing it on to the next generation.

For the first time since it was written, young Americans are now learning the history behind the familiar words, and this will help keep the Pledge alive. But, learning its history—why it was written in 1892, why it was changed in 1923 and 1924 and why "under God" was added in 1954—also helps us understand the important role patriotism plays in strengthening America. And anything that unites and strengthens America will help keep the flame of freedom burning for many more years to come.

APPENDIX

ON AUGUST 20, 1954, CONGRESSMAN LOUIS C. RABAUT MADE THE FOLLOWING REMARKS TO CONGRESS CONCERNING THE ADDITION OF THE PHRASE "UNDER GOD" TO THE PLEDGE OF ALLEGIANCE:

... one of our most devoted and articulate American patriots once said that what we obtain too cheaply we esteem too lightly. May we, as present-day Americans, never forget our sacred traditions and the incomparable and religious nature of our heritage. "Under God" in the Pledge of Allegiance to the flag expresses, aptly and forcefully, a grateful nation's attitude of dependence upon Almighty God. Certainly the spirit of the change should inspire and permeate every loyal citizen, no matter how humble or great his origin.

For under God this Nation lives.

My reason for introducing this resolution may be briefly stated. The most fundamental fact of this moment of history is that the principles of democratic government are being put to the test. The theory as to the nature of man which is the keystone in the arch of American Government is under attack by a system whose philosophy is exactly the opposite. This conflict may be waged with the material implements of war, either hot or cold, but ultimately it will be won by the system of government which is founded upon true and lasting principles, and whose people cling to those principles regardless of the sacrifices entailed. "We are a religious people," said Mr. Justice Douglas, of the United States Supreme Court, in a recent decision "whose institutions presuppose a Supreme Being." This is true in a very fundamental sense. Our political institutions reflect the traditional American conviction of the worthwhileness of the individual human being. That conviction, in turn, is based on our belief that the human person is important because he has been created in the image and likeness of God and that he has been endowed by God with certain inalienable rights which no civil authority may usurp. These principles of the worthwhileness of the individual human being are meaningless unless there exists a Supreme Being.

That is why, in four separate places in our Declaration of Independence the fathers of our Nation referred to God, justifying, by the law of nature and nature's God, the aspiration of the Thirteen Colonies to the status of an independent nation, invoking the Supreme Judge of the world to determine the rectitude of their actions, and seeking the blessings of divine providence on their undertaking. Truly, therefore, this Nation is founded under God.

Now, in our pledge of allegiance to the flag, we salute the symbol of this Republic, and I think it most proper that this pledge express everything for which this Republic stands. The pledge is a reaffirmation of our love of country, of our devotion to an institution that finds its origin and development in the moral law and commands our respect and allegiance so long as it provides that "liberty and justice for all" in which free men can work out their own immortal destinies.

You know and I know that the Union of Soviet Socialist Republics would not, and could not, while supporting the philosophy of communism, place in its patriotic ritual an acknowledgement that their nation existed under God. Indeed, the one fundamental issue which is the unbridgeable gap between America and Communist Russia is belief in Almighty God.

By the addition of the phrase "under God" to the pledge of allegiance the consciousness of the American people will be more alerted to the true meaning of our country and its form of government. In this full awareness we will, I believe, be strengthened for the conflict now facing us and more determined to preserve our precious heritage. More importantly, the children of our land, in the regular recitation of the pledge in school, will be daily impressed with a true understanding of our way of life and its origins. As they grow and advance in this understanding, they will assume the responsibilities of self-government equipped to carry on the traditions that have been given to us. Fortify our youth in their allegiance to the flag by their dedication to one nation under God.

REMARKS BY
SENATOR HOMER FERGUSON
UPON INTRODUCING THE BILL TO ADD
"UNDER GOD" TO THE
PLEDGE OF ALLEGIANCE
February 10, 1954

I believe this modification of the Pledge is important because it highlights one of the real fundamental differences between the free world and the Communist world, namely, belief in God.

Our Nation is founded on a fundamental belief in God, and the first and most important reason for the existence of our Government is to protect the God-given rights of our citizens.

Communism, on the contrary, rejects the very existence of God.

Spiritual values are every bit as important to the defense and safety of our Nation as are military and economic values. America must be defended by the spiritual values which exist in the hearts and souls of the American people. Our country cannot be defended by ships, planes, and guns alone.

In fact, we have an infinite lead over the Communists, in terms of our spiritual and moral values because of our firm belief in God, and because of the spiritual bankruptcy of the Communists.

Indeed, Mr. President, over one of the doorways to this very Chamber inscribed in the marble are the words, "In God we trust." Unless those words amount to more than a carving in stone, our country will never be able to defend itself. Those words must have a very real meaning in the heart of every American.

PRAYER

The following prayer was offered by Reverend Walter A. Mitchell, Pastor of Fountain Memorial Baptist Church in Washington, D.C., on June 14, 1954, the day the Pledge of Allegiance was recited for the first time with the phrase, "under God."

Our loving Heavenly Father, we praise Thee for all the wonderful memories of what this Flag Day stands for in the life of our country. May the flag of our great Nation continue to wave as an emblem of freedom, democracy and Christian principles upon which our beloved Nation has been founded.

Our gracious Father, let these days be days when all Members of this House shall personally dedicate their very best to the tremendous task to which they have been called. And let this be a time when, on the right hand and on the left, men and women shall honestly and sincerely seek to know and to do the will of God in every responsibility.

Teach us the courage of patience, the strength of endurance, and the real power of self restraint as is admonished in the Scriptures:

Let us lay aside every weight and the sin which doth so easily beset us and let us run with patience the race that is set before us, looking unto Jesus the author and finisher of our faith.

In whose name we pray. Amen.

HOW YOU CAN HELP SAVE
THE PLEDGE OF ALLEGIANCE
INVITE TRICIA RAYMOND TO SPEAK TO YOUR GROUP

Tricia Raymond has been informing audiences about the history of the Pledge of Allegiance since 2007. Her patriotic presentation is as inspiring as it is educational.

If you would like to invite Tricia to speak to your group, please feel free to contact her at libertyaloud@gmail.com or visit her website, www.libertyaloud.com.

HERE'S WHAT PEOPLE SAY AFTER HEARING TRICIA:

"Tricia was one of the most knowledgeable people I've had the pleasure of hearing. . . . Her ability to captivate our interest and make those facts and history come to life . . . is what impressed me most."
~Gary C.

"Your information is soooooo interesting." Dot W.

"I was genuinely entertained and informed with your presentation and I know others will be as well." Mark M.

"I thought your presentation on the Pledge of Allegiance was excellent." Pat D.

"Tricia, the program was wonderful." Minnie P.

"Thank you for all the long hours and hard work you have put into this great presentation." Jane V.

JOIN THE RESOLUTION!

2014 is the 60th anniversary of the addition of "under God" to the Pledge of Allegiance.

Find out how you can join thousands of other Americans in recognizing this Important date in our history by going to www.libertyaloud.com and clicking on JOIN THE RESOLUTION!

GLOSSARY

Page 2

cul·mi·nate [**kuhl**-m*uh*-neyt]   To end or arrive at a final stage

Page 3

land·scape [**land**-skeyp]   An expanse of scenery that can be seen in a single view

Page 4

ten·e·ment [**ten**-*uh*-m*uh*nt]   A run-down and often overcrowded apartment house, esp. in a poor section of a large city

hand·craft·ed, hand·craft·ing [**hand**-krafted]   To fashion or make by hand

In·dus·tri·al Re·vo·lu·tion [in-**duhs**-tree-*uh*l / rev-*uh*-**loo**-sh*uh*n] Period of time in which there was a shift from home-based manufacturing to large-scale factory production

Page 5

home·land [**hohm**-land, -l*uh*nd]   One's native land

fam·ine [**fam**-in]   Extreme hunger; starvation

im·mi·grant [**im**-i-gr*uh*nt]   A person who migrates to another country, usually permanently

Page 6

re·sent·ment [ri-**zent**-m*uh*nt]   A feeling of deep and bitter anger

fes·ter [**fes**-ter]   To rankle, as a feeling of resentment

Page 9

strat·e·gy [**strat**-i-jee]   A plan, method, or series of maneuvers for obtaining a specific goal or result

inaugural address [in-**aw**-gyer-*uh*l, -ger-*uh*l / *uh*-**dres**, **ad**-res]   An address delivered at an inaugural ceremony (especially by a United States president)

mal·ice [**mal**-is]   Desire to inflict injury, harm, or suffering on another out of deep-seated meanness

Page 11

as·sas·si·nate [*uh*-**sas**-*uh*-neyt]   To kill suddenly or secretively, especially a politically prominent person; murder premeditatedly and treacherously

Page 12

cam·paign [kam-**peyn**]   A systematic plan of activities for some specific purpose

Page 13

en·vi·sion [en-**vizh**-*uh*n]   To picture mentally, especially some future event

si·mul·ta·ne·ous [sahy-m*uh*l-**tey**-nee-*uh*s]   Existing, occurring, or operating at the same time

Page 27

me·mo·ri·al·ize [m*uh*-**mawr**-ee-*uh*-lahyz]   To provide a memorial for a person or event

Page 28

sar·sa·pa·ril·la [sas-p*uh*-**ril**-*uh*]   A soft drink flavored with an extract of the sarsaparil-la root, as root beer

ef·fec·tu·al [i-**fek**-choo-*uh*l]   Effective

bil·ious [**bil**-y*uh*s]   Indigestion

Page 29

com·mem·o·rate [k*uh*-**mem**-*uh*-reyt]   To honor the memory of by some observance

Page 30

pre·em·i·nent [pree-**em**-*uh*-n*uh*nt]   Superior

Page 34

res·o·lu·tion [rez-*uh*-**loo**-sh*uh*n]   A formal expression of opinion, usually after voting by a legislature

Page 38

u·nani·mous [yoo-**nan**-*uh*-m*uh*s]   Complete agreement

Page 42

typographical error [tahy-p*uh*-**graf**-ik-uhl / er-er]   A mistake in printing, typesetting, or typing, especially one caused by striking an incorrect key on a keyboard.

dis·crep·an·cy [di-**skrep**-*uh*n-see]   An instance of difference or inconsistency

Page 47

gran·deur [**gran**-jer, -j*oo*r]   The quality or state of being impressive or awesome

Page 49

em·bod·y [em-**bod**-ee]   Express

Page 50
Pomp and circumstance [pomp / **sur**-k*uh* m-stans]   Splendid celebration

Page 51
pro·cras·ti·nate [proh-**kras**-t*uh*-neyt, pr*uh*–]   To put off till another day or time
draft [draft, drahft]   A first or preliminary form of any writing, subject to revision, copying, etc.

Page 52
dic·tate [dik-teyt, dik-**teyt**]   To say or read aloud something to be written down by a person or recorded by a machine.
tran·spire [tran-**spahyr**]   Take place

Page 54
de·but [dey-**byoo**, **dey**-byoo, **deb**-yoo]   The first appearance of something, as a new product

Page 55
sal·u·ta·tion [sal-y*uh*-**tey**-sh*uh*]   A word or phrase serving as the preliminary greeting

Page 58
Cath·o·lic [kath-*uh*-lik, **kath**-lik]   Pertaining to the Roman Catholic Church
Flag·staff [**flag**-staf, –stahf]   Flag pole

Page 63
thrive [thrahyv]   Flourish

Page 67
le·git·i·ma·cy [li-**jit**-*uh*-m*uh*-see]   Lawfulness by virtue of being authorized or in accordance with law; undisputed credibility

Page 72
con·tem·plate [kon-t*uh*m-pleyt]   To observe or study thoughtfully
ma·te·ri·al·ist·ic [m*uh*-**teer**-ee-*uh*-list]   Being more concerned with material things than with spiritual, educational, or cultural values
ap·pal [*uh*-**pawl**]   Shock
pros·pect [**pros**-pekt]   Outlook for the future
som·ber [**som**-ber]   Extremely serious
tran·scend·ence [tran-**sen**-d*uh*ns]   Preeminent or supreme

Photo Credits

Page 3   "A One-Sided Bargain" by E.L. Hunt. Printed with permission of the New York State Museum, Albany, NY 12230

Page 4   View of Hester Street from Clinton Street, 1890. Photograph by Brown Brothers, Museum of the City of New York, Print Archives

Page 5   Paul Thompson/National Geographic Image Collection (Top)
                Library of Congress, Prints & Photographs Division, LC-USZ62-11202 (Middle)
                Photography Collection, Miriam and Ira D. Wallach Division of Art, Prints and Photographs, The New York Public Library, Astor, Lenox and Tilden Foundations (Bottom)

Page 6   Library of Congress, Prints & Photographs Division, LC-BH82-2417 (Left)
                Library of Congress, Prints & Photographs Division, LC-BH82-2417(Right)

Page 10   Library of Congress, Prints & Photographs Division, LC-USA7-16837

Pgs 12 & 33   Illustrations by Stephanie R. Holtz

Page 22   Back cover, *The Patriotic Primer for Little Citizens*, 1898, third edition, revised

Pgs 24 & 25   Library of Congress, Prints & Photographs Division, LC-USZ62-65770

Pgs 30 & 60   President Benjamin Harrison Home, Indianapolis

Page 39   Department of Rare Books and Special Collections, University of Rochester Library

Page 43   Courtesy of Rare Books Department, Boston Public Library

Page 48   Department of Rare Books and Special Collections, University of Rochester Library

Page 51   Department of Rare Books and Special Collections, University of Rochester Library

Page 59   Milstein Division of United States History, Local History & Genealogy, The New York Public Library, Astor, Lenox and Tilden Foundations

Page 61   Department of Rare Books and Special Collections, University of Rochester Library

Page 63   Library of Congress, Prints & Photographs Division, LC-USZ62-132420

Page 66   Library of Congress, Prints & Photographs Division, LC-USZ62-14693 (Top)
                Library of Congress, Prints & Photographs Division, LC-USW3-021733-C (Bottom)

Page 71   Homer Ferguson Collection, 23, Senate, Colleagues and Friends, Bentley Historical Library, University of Michigan

Page 72   Courtesy Dwight D. Eisenhower Library

Pages 1, 2, 7, 11, 13—21, 23, 27, 31, 34—37, 41, 43, 44, 47, 49, and 53—55 are compiled from the J.D. Williams Library, University of Mississippi.

Acknowledgments

Many people helped make this book a reality and I owe a debt of gratitude to each of them. To Jan Bloom, my distant friend and mentor, a special mention of appreciation for showing me it could be done. To my good friend and former boss, Erskine Wells, a sincere thank-you for encouraging me along the way.

For special help researching the images included in this book, I'd like to thank the following: Melanie Bower, Museum of the City of New York; Jennifer Capps, curator with the President Benjamin Harrison Home Foundation; Sean Casey, Boston Public Library; Bonnie Coles, Library of Congress; Faye Haun, Museum of the City of New York; Thomas Lisanti, The New York Public Library; Melissa Mead, University of Rochester; and Ashley Morton, National Geographic Society.

A special note of gratitude goes to the Eudora Welty Library's staff in Jackson, MS, an incredibly competent and committed group of people, specifically Charlie Brenner, Interlibrary Loan Manager, and Michelle Hudson, Reference Librarian, for their patient assistance.

And finally, thank you also to Mrs. August Amato, daughter of Louis C. Rabaut, for sharing the 1954 "Under God" poster.